RAINBOW

Travel Through
The Caribbean

Lynn Huggins-Cooper

QEB Publishing

First published in the United States by
QEB Publishing, Inc.
23062 La Cadena Drive
Laguna Hills, CA 92653

www.qeb-publishing.com

Library of Congress Control Number: 2007000940

ISBN 978 1 59566 355 9

Written by Lynn Huggins-Cooper
Designed by Manishi Varshney (Q2A Media)
Editor Honor Head
Picture Researcher Rituparna Sengupta/Lalit Dalal (Q2A Media)

Publisher Steve Evans
Creative Director Zeta Davies
Senior Editor Hannah Ray

Printed and bound in China

Words in **bold** can be found in the glossary on page 31.

Contents

Where in the world is the Caribbean? 5

What is the Caribbean like? 6

Climate 8

Getting around 10

Major cities 12

Farming 14

Food and drink 16

Island history 18

Pirates of the Caribbean 20

Tourism 22

Festivals and holidays 24

Environmental issues 26

Activity ideas 28

Glossary 31

Index 32

Florida

North Atlantic
Ocean

Andros
Island

Bahamas

Isla de la
Juventud

Cuba

Virgin
Islands

Anguilla

St. Martin

St.-Barthélemy

Cayman Islands

Haiti

Dominican
Republic

Antigua and
Barbuda

Jamaica

Puerto Rico

Virgin
Islands

St Kitts
and Nevis

Caribbean Sea

Montserrat

Dominica

Guadeloupe

St. Lucia

Honduras

Barbados

Nicaragua

St. Vincent and
the Grenadines

Grenada

Trinidad
and Tobago

Costa
Rica

Colombia

Panama

Venezuela

Where in the world is the Caribbean?

The Caribbean is a collection of islands found in the region southeast of North America, to the north and west of South America, and east of Central America. The **archipelago** is made up of more than 7,000 islands stretching 2,600 mi. (4,184 km) between Florida and Venezuela. Although they are all part of the Caribbean, each island has its own culture and traditions, so a journey through the Caribbean can be very exciting. Most of the islands have people living on them. Some of the islands are owned by other countries such as Britain, France, the Netherlands, and the USA. Some are even owned by very rich people, such as Little Whale Cay in the Bahamas. It is possible to rent some of these tiny islands for a vacation.

The Caribbean includes islands such as Cuba, Hispaniola, Puerto Rico, Jamaica, Trinidad, Tobago, the Bahamas, the Virgin Islands, Dominica, Antigua, St. Lucia, Belize, Barbados, Haiti—and many, many more!

Did you know?

OFFICIAL NAME: the Caribbean

LOCATION: Western hemisphere, southeast Americas

SURROUNDING COUNTRIES: North America, Central America, South America

SURROUNDING SEAS AND OCEANS: Caribbean Sea, Atlantic Ocean

CAPITALS: Havana (Cuba); Santo Domingo (Dominican Republic); San Juan (Puerto Rico); Kingston (Jamaica)

AREA: 89,604 sq. mi. (232,074 sq. km)

POPULATION: 39,239,636

LIFE EXPECTANCY: about 71 years

RELIGIONS: Rastafari, Haitian Voudoun, Cuban Santeria, Spiritual Baptist

LANGUAGES: Many, including Dutch, Papiamento, English, and Spanish

CLIMATE: **tropical**

HIGHEST MOUNTAIN: Pico Duarte in the Dominican Republic 10, 164 ft. (3,098 m) high

MAJOR RIVERS: Cauto (Cuba, 230 mi./370 km long); Río Artibonito (Hispaniola, 149 mi./240 km long); Rio Minho (Jamaica, 57 mi./92.5 km long); Grande de Arecibo (Puerto Rico, 34 mi./55 km long)

CURRENCIES: Many, including dollars, euros, and florins

What is the Caribbean like?

Throughout the Caribbean there are many different types of landscapes, from **cloud forests** to volcanic mountains, **mangrove** swamps, deserts, and rain forests. **Conservation International** sees the Caribbean as a hotspot for **biodiversity**—that means there are huge numbers of different types of animals and plants found there.

The Arenal volcano in Rincon de la Vieja National Park, Costa Rica, has been constantly erupting since 1968.

The sand on Pink Beach, Harbor Island, is tinted a delicate pink color because it contains tiny pieces of coral.

Pink sand

The Caribbean is made up of many islands, so there is a great deal of coast to visit, with many coves and long, sandy beaches. The beautiful Pink Beach on Harbor Island in the Bahamas is said to be the most photographed beach in the world. In some places in the Caribbean, such as St. Lucia, the sand is black because it is made from tiny pieces of volcanic lava.

Mount Roraima in Venezuela was the inspiration for Sir Arthur Conan Doyle's book *The Lost World.*

Big and small

Some of the islands are very tiny, such as St. Martin with an area of only 37 sq. mi. (96 sq. km). Others are much larger, such as Cuba, with an area of 42,803 sq. mi. (110,860 sq. km). The population of the Caribbean tends to be concentrated on particular islands. Cuba, for example, has a population of 11,382,820. Some of the smaller islands have very few people living on them, such as Montserrat, with a population of only 4,000.

West Indies

Some parts of the Caribbean are called the West Indies. This is because an Italian explorer named **Christopher Columbus** (1451–1506) called the islands the Indies because he thought he had landed in India. When he realized his mistake, the name was changed to the West Indies, so people wouldn't be confused with the East Indies, now called Indonesia.

Many people vacation on cruise ships visiting the islands that make up the Caribbean.

Climate

The **climate** in most areas of the Caribbean is tropical, and as a result many beautiful and exotic plants, such as orchids, grow on the islands. A tropical climate means that you should be prepared for hot and damp conditions. You should also take plenty of high-factor sunscreen with you because the sun is very strong. The temperature doesn't vary much between the hottest and coolest months, with temperatures of around 82°F (28°C) in July to August and around 75°F (24°C) in January to February. One of the reasons that the Caribbean is popular with tourists is because there is so much sunshine, with seven to nine hours on most days.

Warm, clear water full of brightly colored fish makes diving and snorkeling popular.

I love living in the Caribbean. After school, I spend time on the beach and buy fruit and cool drinks from the beach stalls. I go snorkeling with my friends, and the water is so clear and blue it almost doesn't look real. Sometimes, I feel as though I am in a wildlife documentary, as I see the coral with tiny, brightly colored fish darting in and out. My favorite sea creatures are the rays that float about as though they are flying!
Elmino

Many orchids and other exotic plants grow wild in the warm temperatures of the Caribbean.

Stormy weather

The Caribbean sometimes experiences **hurricanes**. These are terrible storms that can cause a lot of damage to property and can be dangerous to people and animals. The hurricane season is from June to November, but most hurricanes happen in September. Wind speeds during a hurricane can reach up to 149 mph. (240 kph).

In the mountains

There is some variation in climate across the Caribbean. In Cuba and the northern islands of the Bahamas, winter temperatures sometimes fall to around 59°F (15°C), but this is still warm and pleasant. Where there are mountainous regions, such as the Blue Mountains in Jamaica, the weather can be much colder.

Hurricane Hugo caused a great deal of damage in the Caribbean in 1989.

Getting around

Once you arrive in the Caribbean, there are many ways to travel between the islands because lots of them are so close together. A trip that takes in a lot of different islands is often called "island-hopping." Some visitors to the Caribbean like to take a cruise, so they can visit many islands in one trip.

Sea and air

Regional airlines take visitors to many different islands on small planes. Some tiny planes can land on water—these are called seaplanes. The planes often fly low, so you can see the beautiful views below as you travel. There are also different types of inter-island ferries, from old-fashioned **schooners** to modern **hydrofoils** that shoot across the water at high speeds.

Many people like to take sailing vacations around the Caribbean islands on schooners.

It's spring break and I'm having a great time visiting different islands. I have been on a beautiful old schooner, which made me feel as though I'd stepped into a film set. It was 79 ft. (24 m) long and had huge, white sails that billowed in the wind. It had a diesel engine, too, in case the wind dropped. Mom and I also took a trip in a tiny seaplane. The views were amazing. We saw sharks swimming across the reef! I felt a little worried as we landed at the quay on the tiny island, and bobbing up and down as we got off was quite scary, but it's a really fun way to travel!
Grace

Seaplanes can land on water because they have special pontoons underneath.

Bikes are a popular way to explore many of the smaller Caribbean islands.

On your bike!

Because so many of the islands are small, the local people get around on mopeds and bikes, as well as by using cars. If you visit a Caribbean island, you can often rent mountain bikes from larger hotels. This is a great way to see the sights and keep in shape at the same time. Larger islands have good bus networks, especially in the cities. Riding on the buses means you can meet the local people as you travel—though the buses do get very full.

Major cities

Although visitors tend to come to the Caribbean for the spectacular beaches, the stunning scenery, and the glorious weather, there are also some interesting towns and cities to explore. Kingston is the capital of Jamaica. It has two areas: Downtown, which is the oldest part of Kingston and which has many historic buildings; and New Kingston, with visitor attractions such as the Bob Marley Museum. Bob Marley was one of the world's most popular **reggae** artists, and the museum is the house in which he lived when he was alive.

Port Royal was known as the "richest and wickedest city on Earth" because it was a safe place for pirates to hide after they had attacked a ship.

Old capital

Port Royal was Jamaica's previous capital city, and was on the top of the **peninsula** that borders the harbor. A museum there tells the story of how Port Royal was submerged under the sea after an earthquake in 1692.

The Bob Marley Museum is in the house where the musician lived and founded a record label called Tuff Gong along with his band, The Wailers.

Historical place

Santo Domingo in the Dominican Republic is a beautiful, historic city. Many buildings there date back to the 1500s, including the Cathedral Basilica Santa Maria la Menor. Visitors also love the dance clubs where they can **merengue** and **salsa**. One of the most impressive clubs is the Guácara Taina, which is in a massive, natural underground cave.

This club is in a cave 49 ft. (15 m) below the ground.

The original Santo Domingo was a walled city that is now part of the larger modern city.

Beautiful gardens

The Hope Botanical Gardens in Kingston are a wonderful place to visit, and you can see many beautiful orchids growing there. You can also visit the White Marl Arawak Museum, and see **artifacts** that belonged to the Arawak Indians, who were the first people to live in Jamaica.

We went to the Hope Botanical Gardens today. There were orchids growing wild, just like the pink ones Granny grows as houseplants. I learned that **crops**, such as pineapple, **cocoa**, and coffee were introduced to Jamaica by being first grown in the gardens.
Love, Sam

Farming

Because the Caribbean islands are so warm, farmers can grow a **huge** variety of crops, both for local people to eat fresh and for **export**. Crops grown for the **local** people to eat include yams, avocados, pumpkins, and peppers. Foods grown for export include bananas, sugar, coffee, cocoa, oranges, grapefruits, tangerines, coconuts, and spices, such as pimento, from which the seasoning allspice is made.

Sweet potatoes

Avocados

Fruit and vegetables grown in the Caribbean are flown all over the world to be sold in shops and supermarkets.

Sweet peppers

Pumpkins

At school this week, we learned about Fairtrade projects. We were all really interested in how Fairtrade chocolate is made. I didn't realize that so many cocoa farmers around the world were very poor. We found out that you can now buy chocolate, drinking chocolate, and cocoa that has been grown and produced in fair circumstances, which means the farmers are paid a proper price for their cocoa beans.
Ruby

Cocoa beans are left out in the sun to dry in large trays. The lady walking in the beans is turning them as they dry.

Fairtrade farms

Some farmers are part of Fairtrade schemes. That means the farmers are paid a fair price for the goods they produce, rather than all the money going to people from other countries who **import** and sell the food. A fair price for their goods means the farmers do not have to live in poverty anymore. There is a Fairtrade group of 42 cocoa farmers in the Dominican Republic, called the Conacado cooperative. The cooperative helps farmers work together as a group to sell part of its crop to the Fairtrade market. The farmers receive a guaranteed minimum price for their goods and a bonus, which is spent on the whole community.

Fairtrade schemes help whole communities because the money earned helps pay for schools, medical care, and better housing.

15

Food and drink

Caribbean food includes lots of fish caught in the warm waters that surround the islands, and the delicious fruits and vegetables that grow in the hot, tropical climate.

Ackee is a very popular breakfast in many parts of the Caribbean.

Favorite dishes

Ackee and salt fish is the national dish of Jamaica and is often eaten for breakfast. It is made of salt fish (fish preserved in salt), ackee, onions, tomatoes, peppers, and pork fat all mixed up together. Ackee is a fruit that has many poisonous parts, so this dish is prepared very carefully. Another popular Caribbean dish is "jerk" —chicken or pork slow-cooked over a flame. It is said to have come from when Maroons, escaped Jamaican slaves, cooked meat over open fires. Jerk uses peppers, pimento seeds, thyme, and nutmeg for flavor and is cooked over hot coals covered with the branches of pimento or allspice wood.

Jerk meat is a traditional Caribbean food and is sold in Caribbean restaurants around the world.

Callaloo and fungi

You'll find this dish in the Virgin Islands. Callaloo is like spinach soup or stew and it is cooked with crabs, **okra**, and hot pepper sauce. Fungi has nothing to do with mushrooms, which you might expect. It is cornmeal and looks a bit like couscous or rice. It is served with callaloo to soak up the juices.

Sugar cane

Sugar cane is grown in the Caribbean. The sugar drips out of it as a kind of syrup. You can cut off the top of a cane and suck out the syrup. The local people use it to make cakes, pies, and sweet fried dumplings as well as rum cake—a sponge soaked with rum.

Sugar cane used to be grown on large **plantations**. All the work was done by slaves. Today, sugar cane is grown for use by local people as well as to be made into sugar for export.

Island history

The Arawak, Carib, and Taino Indians lived in the Caribbean long before Europeans arrived on the islands. They are now known as the **First Peoples**. The Arawak Indians were the first people that Christopher Columbus met when he came to the Caribbean. He landed on the island now called the Bahamas. These **indigenous** peoples were treated harshly by the explorers and settlers who came to the Caribbean, and many of them died.

These ancient paintings were made by Arawak people. They are in the Fontein Cave in the Arikok National Park on the island of Aruba.

This traditional windmill is on an old plantation on the Caribbean island of St. Croix.

The First People

If you visit the Caribbean, you can see many museums that tell the story of the First Peoples. In Jamaica, you can visit the Coyaba River Garden Museum. In the town of Ocho Rios, you can go to the Arawak Museum, and you can visit the White Marl Taino Museum in Kingston. You can also visit the Green Grotto Caves, where you can see preserved cave drawings. In Cuba, you can see Arawak remains in the Montane Museum.

Historical buildings

There are many buildings that were built by the invaders and settlers who **colonized** the Caribbean, such as the English, Spanish, Dutch, and French. You can see churches and cathedrals, ruined fortifications, plantation houses, and burial grounds.

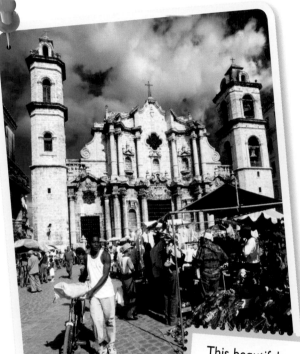

This beautiful cathedral, Catedral de San Cristóbal de La Habana, was built in Havana in 1724.

I have been finding out all about the Taino people, some of the First Peoples who lived in the Caribbean. I was amazed to discover that the Spanish explorers who came to the Bahamas, Cuba, and Hispaniola in 1492 were all men. They had children with Taino women and many people in the Caribbean are descended from the First Peoples.
Marlee

Terrible history

Across the Caribbean, African slaves were brought by the white settlers to work on their huge farms, called plantations. The slaves lived terrible lives and were treated very badly. There are many people living in the Caribbean today who are descendants of those slaves. The slaves influenced the language, religion, and festivals of the Caribbean, bringing African traditions to the islands.

Pirates of the Caribbean

From the 1500s to the 1700s, the Caribbean was a haven for pirates, with thousands of coves and bays to hide in and even whole "pirate towns" in which to spend their treasure! For example, the island of Tortuga was a pirate hideout for many years, until around 1688. Pirate raids were carried out on Spanish ships as they moored off Cuba on their way to Spain.

Perfect for pirates

New Providence, in the Bahamas, was another pirate stronghold in the 1670s. It had a shallow harbor that pirate ships could travel into safely, but which was too small for warships to follow. The **trade lanes** between Europe and the West Indies offered rich pickings for pirates as they plundered ships and then sailed away to hide in the many coves and bays. Lots of famous pirates visited the Bahamas, such as Blackbeard, Calico Jack Rackham, and the infamous female pirate Anne Bonney.

Fort Fincastle in Nassau was built in 1793. It was a lookout point to protect the island from pirates.

Kidnapped!

If you go to Santiago de Cuba, you can visit the Piracy Museum in the Morro Castle. It is a fortress built in the 17th century, high on a cliff over the bay. Between 1538 and 1562, Santiago de Cuba was the victim of terrible pirate attacks. The pirate Jacques de Sores attacked the city in the middle of the night, kidnapping people and holding them to ransom. The townsfolk decided they'd had enough and moved to Bayamo, away from the coast.

El Castillo del Morro (the Morro Castle) was built in 1539 by Spanish settlers to guard the entrance to San Juan bay from pirates and enemy ships.

YOU'VE GOT MAIL

At school, we did a project on Port Royal. My class went on a pirate trail. I dressed up as Anne Bonney, the fierce pirate. I learned how the pirates fought with cutlasses—sharp swords. My friend Alex dressed as Blackbeard and even had a big false beard!
Love,
Sonia

Tourism

The Caribbean is a hugely popular holiday destination for visitors from all over the world. In particular, there are many tourists from North America, which is very close to the Caribbean.

Global warming is making sea temperatures rise, and coral reefs are dying as a result.

Ecotourism

Ecotourism describes vacations to beautiful, natural places, such as forests and beaches, where the tourists try to protect the places they are visiting. This is becoming popular in the Caribbean, with its rich and varied landscapes and wildlife. Many people come to the Caribbean to visit the beaches, and enjoy scuba diving on coral reefs. You can see **marlin**, porpoises, sharks, and sea turtles as well as tiny, colorful reef fish. You may like to book a boat trip to watch huge, gentle whales swim by. Some people come for longer working vacations to help environmental projects preserve wildlife and animal habitats. You can also go on rain forest tours, staying in **eco lodges**, and trekking out into the jungle, watching brightly colored birds in the **canopy**.

You must never touch the coral on a reef or it will be damaged and die.

Cruising the seas

Caribbean cruises are very popular luxury vacations because they give travelers the chance to explore a variety of islands. Many large cruise liners begin their Caribbean voyages from the southern end of North America. The ships are like floating hotels, with restaurants, discos, stores, gyms, spas, play areas, and swimming pools.

Many tourists visit Turtle Beach in the town of Ochos Rios, Jamaica.

Do you like the photo of the bugs on this postcard? They are leaf-cutter ants. We saw them marching along vines in the rain forest in Costa Rica. They were carrying pieces of leaf much bigger than themselves. I also loved the spider monkeys that leapt backward and forward across the vines above our lodge, but they were really noisy! Our guide said we should be careful not to wear yellow because not only does yellow attract insects, but it also makes the monkeys likely to spray you with pee. I wore my blue T-shirt!

Jamie

A leaf-cutter ant colony can contain up to eight million ants!

Festivals and holidays

The Caribbean has many festivals and holidays because settlers from different places have brought their traditions with them. However, all the celebrations have a few things in common—color, fun, and great food!

Junkanoo is a street festival held in the Bahamas on December 26th and January 1st.

Carnival

All over the Caribbean, Carnival, Carnaval, or Carnavale is celebrated in spring. It began as a Christian festival at the beginning of Lent, the period that leads up to Easter. Today, massive celebrations are held, with parades, decorated floats, **steel pan drums**, and street dancing. One of the best things about Carnival is the amazing costumes. Some of them have huge frames, made by bending wire and canes into all sorts of shapes, such as butterfly wings. The frames are covered in fabric, paper, plastic, and, of course, a lot of glitter and sequins. Many of the costumes are huge, but the person wearing the costume still needs to be able to dance!

Steel pan drums are traditionally made from huge barrels that contained oil.

People spend months making the beautiful costumes they wear at Carnival time.

I can't believe that it's almost time for Carnival again. Only three weeks now—I can't wait! Mom has been making the wings for my butterfly costume for months—she's sewn on loads of sequins. She's going as a black widow spider. She looks great, but Dad's a bit worried!
Love,
Betty x

Saut d'Eau

In Haiti, there is a festival called Saut d'Eau. Saut d'Eau is a well and waterfall where it is believed that an image of the Virgin Mary appeared in the 1800s. Today, many **pilgrims** pray to the Voudoun goddess of love—Erzulie. People walk a long way to visit the waterfall, where they bathe in the waters as drummers play music. There is a feast and prayers are said.

Environmental issues

The Caribbean has many fabulous natural resources, from crystal clear water and beautiful cloud forests to rain forests teeming with animal life. This attracts visitors who want to experience all the beauty firsthand, but that can cause problems. The more visitors who want to come, the more likely it is that the environment will be damaged. If there are more tourists, more hotels, resorts, and facilities need to be built to accommodate them.

Widespread destruction

All this development can lead to the destruction of animal habitats and pollution. Many Caribbean islands are taking steps to protect their wildlife and habitats, and there are many national parks full of animals and plants, such as passion flowers, orchids, and hibiscus. The British Virgin Islands have 17 protected national parks, including St. Eustatius Marine Park, which has protected areas for endangered leatherback turtles to lay their eggs.

These black–necked stilts enjoy protection in the Palo Verde National Park, in Costa Rica.

Threatened birds

Protection is important because many plant and animal species that live in the Caribbean are very rare. In Dominica, scientists are studying the nesting behavior of threatened Sisserou and Jaco parrots to see what needs to be done to protect them. In Jamaica and the Cayman Islands, the Buffy Flower bat is studied so that they may be protected in the future.

Saving the fish

Marine life in the Caribbean is also protected by not allowing too many fish to be caught for food. Coral reefs and the creatures that live there are protected against being taken from the sea to be sold to tourists as souvenirs.

The Imperial parrot is only found in the mountain rain forest of Dominica and is protected from hunters by law.

I have been studying the Las Baulas National Park on the Pacific coast of Costa Rica. It is where rare leatherback turtles come to nest and lay their eggs. The turtles are counted, and the nests are protected from predators. The beaches are patrolled and guarded to stop people from stealing the eggs and scaring the turtles.
Paul

Leatherback turtles live their whole life—which can be as long as 80 years—at sea. Females return to land only to lay their eggs.

Activity ideas

1 Look at Web sites about the Caribbean. Make a list of twenty islands and find a fact about each one.

2 Using books and the Internet, find out about the creatures that live on coral reefs in the Caribbean. Make a fact file about the plants and creatures who live in and around the reefs.

3 Imagine that you are traveling through the Caribbean. How will you get round? By cruise ship, by sea plane, or maybe by bike? What will you see? Write a journal about your trip.

4 Find out about carnival costumes and masks. Design and make your own mask from thin cardstock decorated with feathers and sequins.

5 Find out more about hurricanes. Write an explanation about how hurricanes are formed.

6 Find recordings of music by reggae artists, such as Bob Marley. While you are listening to the music, paint or draw a bright picture of a sunny Caribbean beach.

7 Plan a vacation to the Caribbean. Which islands would you visit? Which sites would you go and see? Use the Internet and travel brochures to help you plan your trip.

8 Find out more about the Arawak, Carib, and Taino people—the First Peoples of the Caribbean. Describe what happened to them when invaders and settlers, such as the Spanish, English, and Dutch, arrived.

9 Make a model of a leatherback turtle. Stuff a paper bag with cotton for the body, and make the legs and head from cardstock. Tape them onto the bag. Then make a shell from crumpled brown and green crepe paper stuck onto a round cardstock base. Glue the shell to your turtle's body. You could make eggs from white tissue or clay, too!

11 With an adult, visit the supermarket and make a list of all the Fairtrade food that is available. Buy some Fairtrade chocolate and "taste test" it to see how it compares with ordinary brands.

NOTE FOR ADULTS: Please ensure that children do not suffer from any food allergies before carrying out a taste test.

10 Write a story about a leatherback turtle fighting her way ashore to lay her eggs. What dangers does she face? Imagine you are the turtle—what are your feelings? What will happen to your eggs when you return to the sea?

12 Find out more about what life was like for the African people taken to work on plantations in the Caribbean. Research using books in your school library.

13 Find a Caribbean folktale from a book or the Internet. Read it, and then draw illustrations for the story. You could get together with some friends and perform the folktale as a play.

14 Write a leaflet for tourists describing Kingston, Jamaica. Use exciting language so that people are encouraged to visit.

15 Make your own pirate treasure chest. Get an old shoebox and attach the back of the lid to the back of the box with tape to make a hinge. Tape a rectangle of cardstock to the lid, curved over to make it look like a real pirate treasure chest. Cover the box in a few layers of strips of newspaper glued with PVA glue. When your chest has dried, paint it brown and draw on "studs" with a gold pen. Fill it with your pirate treasure!

16 Find a recipe for callaloo in a cookbook or on the Internet. With an adult, try making the dish. If you cannot find all the ingredients, ask an adult to help you to adapt the recipe.

NOTE FOR ADULTS: Please ensure that children do not suffer from any food allergies before making or eating any food.

17 Carry out research using the Internet, magazines, and newspapers to find out more about the problem of water pollution on reefs in the Caribbean. Use the information you find to design a leaflet to tell people about the dangers to the environment.

18 Imagine you are a pirate. Write a journal of your adventures—and don't forget to describe the treasure you find!

19 Look at old pirate maps in books or on the Internet. Age a piece of paper by painting it with tea or coffee and crumpling it up a few times to make it look old. Draw a map with islands, treasure, and sea monsters. Ask an adult to help you to complete the map with a blob of red wax crayon melted on the corner as a seal—press an old pen lid into the soft wax to make an imprint.

Glossary

archipelago A large group of islands

artifacts Objects of historical interest, such as tools, weapons, or ornaments

biodiversity Lots of different plant and animal species found in an environment

canopy The top level of a rain forest

Christopher Columbus An Italian explorer living in the 1400s, who worked for the Spanish kings and queen

climate The usual weather conditions of a particular place or region

cloud forests Tropical forests, often near peaks of coastal mountains, which have cloud cover all year

cocoa Powder made from the seeds of the cacao plant, used in making chocolate

colonized To take over and make your own

Conservation International A group concerned with taking care of the planet

crops Plants or agricultural produce

eco lodges Places where tourists stay, which are friendly to the environment

export Shipping goods to sell in other countries

First Peoples People who are native to a particular place

hurricanes Violent tropical storms

hydrofoils Boats that travel across the water very fast by skimming over the surface

import To bring in goods from another country to sell

indigenous People, animals, or plants that originated In a particular place or country

mangrove A tropical tree that grows in mud and swamps

marlin A large game fish

merengue A ballroom dance from Dominica and Haiti

okra A small, green vegetable

peninsula An area of land almost completely surrounded by water, except it is connected to the mainland

pilgrims People who go on a journey to visit a place for religious reasons

plantations Large farms that used slave labor to produce cotton, sugar, and other crops

reggae A type of music popular across the Caribbean, especially in Jamaica

regional Relating to a particular place or region

salsa A fast ballroom dance, originally from Puerto Rico

schooners Sailing ships with two or more masts

steel pan drum Bowl-shaped percussion instruments common in the Caribbean, made from steel barrels

trade lanes Routes taken by ships to transport goods from place to place

tropical Hot and humid climate

Index

ackee 16
activities 28–30
airlines 10
ants 23
Arawak Indians 13, 18, 29
archipelago 5, 31
artifacts 13, 31
Atlantic Ocean 5

Bahamas 6, 9, 18, 19, 20
beaches 6
bicycles 11
biodiversity 6, 31
birds 26, 27
buildings 19

callaloo 17, 30
canopy 22, 31
Carib Indians 18, 29
Caribbean Sea 5
Carnival 25, 28
cave drawings 18
Cayman Islands 27
cities 12–13
climate 5, 8–9, 31
cloud forests 6, 26, 31

cocoa 13, 31

colonized 19, 31
Columbus, Christopher 7, 18, 31
Conservation International 6, 31
coral reefs 22, 27, 28, 30
Costa Rica 6, 23, 26–27

crops 13, 14, 31
cruises 7, 10, 22
Cuba 7, 9, 18, 19

currencies 5

diving 8, 22
Dominica 27
Dominican Republic 13, 15
Doyle, Sir Arthur Conan 7

eco lodges 22, 31
environment 26–27
export 14, 17, 31

Fairtrade 14–15, 29
farming 14–15
festivals 19, 24–25
First Peoples 18, 19, 29, 31
fish 8, 27
food 16–17, 30
fungi (cornmeal) 17

habitats 22, 26
Harbor Island 6
Havana 19
history 18–19
holidays 24–25
Hope Botanical Gardens 13
hurricanes 9, 28, 31
hydrofoils 10, 31

import 15, 31
indigenous 18, 31
island-hopping 10
islands 5, 6–7, 22

Jamaica 9, 12, 13, 16, 18, 23, 27
jerk meat 16

Junkanoo 24
Kingston 12, 13, 18

landscapes 6
languages 5, 19
leatherback turtles 26, 27, 29
life expectancy 5
location 5

mangroves 6, 31
maps 4, 30
Marley, Bob 12, 28
marlin 22, 31
merengue 13, 31
Montserrat 7
Morro Castle 21
mountains 5, 9
museums 12, 13, 18, 21

Nassau 20
national parks 6, 18, 26
New Providence 20

okra 17, 31
orchids 8–9, 13

peninsula 12, 31
pilgrims 25, 31
pirates 20–21, 30
plantations 17, 18, 19, 29, 31
plants 8
pollution 26, 30
population 5, 7
Port Royal 12

rain forests 22, 23, 26
reggae 12, 28, 31
regional 10, 31
religions 5, 19
rivers 5

St. Croix 18
St. Lucia 6
St. Martin 7
salsa 13, 31
Santa Domingo 13
Santiago de Cuba 21
Saut d'Eau 25
schooners 10, 11, 31
seaplanes 10–11
slaves 19
snorkeling 8
spider monkeys 23
steel pan drum 25, 31
sugar cane 17

Taino Indians 18, 19, 29
Tortuga 20
tourism 8, 22–23
trade lanes 20, 31
transport 10–11
tropical 5, 8, 31

Virgin Islands 17, 26
volcanoes 6–7

West Indies 7

wildlife protection 22, 26-27